INTRODUCTION

The paraphanalia and tricks in this booklet are not new to the amateur magic buff. The author has clothed old magic with a Christian wardrobe.

He, himself, has used them for six decades, and as he nears what Solomon described as 'The long home when the mourners go about the streets' (Eccles. 12) he has sought to pass on to others the propagation of the Good News of the Gospel, which he now feels is no longer in the range of his limited capabilities.

Arnold Carl Westphal
December 1981

PREFACE

The 15th chapter of Luke tells about three things that were lost and found, a sheep, a shekel and a son.

The paraphanalia used in the chapters that follow are among such treasures. They have been stored away in Father Time's attic trunk for several decades, so there is nothing new about the basic objects.

The tricks are old but the truth is new - yet older than the tricks.

To the elderly they will be ancient, but to the young they will be like fresh fruits from a garden sown with the seeds of wonder.

To all they will be like direction - posts, pointing to the Pot of Gold at the end of the rainbow of eternal life.

Build them and use them to God's glory.

GOSPEL MAGIC
HOME MADE
SELF CONTAINED

GOSPEL "SURPRISE" VISUAL AIDS

BY ARNOLD CARL WESTPHAL

DRAWINGS BY CHARLES CAGLE

VISUAL EVANGELS PUBLISHING COMPANY

1401 OHIO STREET

MICHIGAN CITY, INDIANA 46360

 For information address
Visual Evangels Publishers. 1401 Ohio Street
Michigan City, Indiana 46360

FIRST PRINTING 1982

ISBN - 0 - 915398 - 20 - 6

PRINTED IN U.S.A

TABLE OF CONTENTS

CHAPTER 1

THE BROKEN LOVE CORD

". . .sin when it is finished bringeth forth death."
(James 1:15)

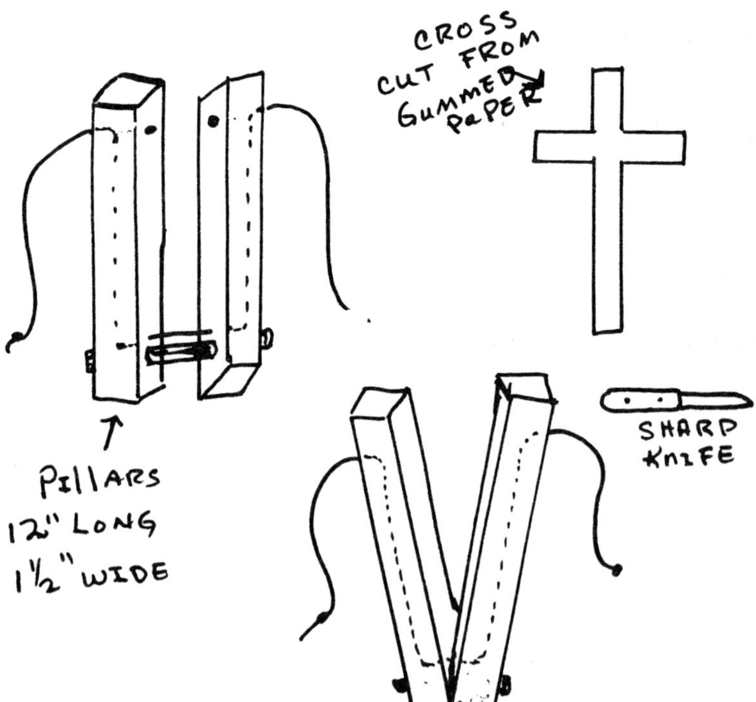

PROPERTY

Two wood pillars 12 inches long and 1½ inches square. a bolt and nut, washers, a thin bladed knife and a cross on gummed paper.

PREPARATION

Drill a hole through the entire length of both pillars. Near the top of the pillars, drill holes through the pillars.. Do the same at the lower end. Then drill a hole through the pillars below the bottom holes and insert the bolt so the pillars can be split. Thread a long cord through the pillars entering at the top hole of one pillar and going to the bottom hole and across to second pillar and out of the top hole of that pillar. Plug up the top and bottom holes of the pillars and glue in some dummy rope in the inside top holes.

PROCEDURE

During the lesson with the pillars closed, pull the cord back and forth. Then go through the act of cutting the cord between the pillars. Split the pillars so the 'damage' can be seen. Put the pillars back together and wrap the gummed cross around the pillars. Pull on the cord, showing it to be restored.

PRESENTATION

(Begin with the pillars side by side and pull on the cord). How wonderful to be made in the image of God, in the image of his holiness and perfection and everlastingness. This is how Adam and Eve started. There was an unbroken love cord between them and God.

The animals did not snarl and bite, the ground had no thorns or thistles, there was no sweat from labor in the garden and pain was unheard of in this Paradise of Peace.

The fruits of the garden were freely harvested and enjoyed to the full but one tree was to remain untouched.

God was like a landlord, saying to his tenant, "You may have free run of my house except one room." A landlord has this right since he is the owner.

THE LOVE CORD IS BROKEN

Then Satan came and skillfully raised doubts in the minds of the caretakers about this tree whose luscious fruit had sharpened the appetites of those who were to become the first parents and from whom all people descended. Adam and Eve were to become the heads of the human race.

But they disobeyed the Creator Landlord and yielded to the temptation to taste the forbidden fruit.

The moment they did, the love cord between them and God was cut. (Put the knife blade between the pillars and open the pillars and show the glued ends of the cord).

THE FIRST SACRIFICE OF BLOOD

Adam and Eve were now frightened. Their sin began to trouble them. They now knew they were naked and they tried to repair the damage by sewing fig leaves together to cover their nakedness.

When God their landlord came, they played like they were not at home by hiding in the garden. God called to them saying, "Adam where art thou?"

Knowing by now that they must give an account for their disobedience and nakedness, they came out of hiding and offered a bagful of excuses. Adam blamed Eve and Eve blamed the serpent. They apologized for their nakedness and explained about the fig leaves as a covering.

Then God ordered them to make coats of skins. Animals were slain and this resulted in the snarling and biting in self defense and it became a way of life in the animal kingdom. Thorns and thistles sprang up in the green carpet of grass and joy in taking care of the garden became hard labor with sweat and weariness. Pain was promised in family life and the serpent was sentenced to crawl on its belly in the dust - all because the love cord was broken

THE ORIGIN OF DEATH

Physical death became a part of the penalty. Since then and until now that penalty has been a sorrowful part of life.

People hate and kill, animals snarl and bite, gardens produce weeds, man works by the sweat of his face and death visits our homes - all because the love cord was broken.

GOD'S PLAN FOR REDEMPTION

But God made immediate plans to defeat the works of Satan who prompted it all. God said, "The seed of the woman will one day bruise the head of the serpent for the bite of the serpent has wounded the heel of man." (Gen. 3:15).

(Hold up the cross). In the meantime Jesus came to complete God's plan, because God so loved the world that he gave his only begotten Son, that whosoever believeth might have everlasting life. (John 3:16). God sent not his Son into the world to condemn the world but that the world might be saved. (John 3:18).

CHRIST IS THE ANSWER

(Close the pillars and wrap the cross around them).

Though the world still thrives on sin, love overshadows and the way is open to restore the broken love cord. (Pull on the cord and show restoration). It is the way of the cross that leads home.

As the Apostle Paul pondered the mercy of God, he wrote, "Where sin abounded, grace did much more."

John wrote, "We have fellowship, one with another and the blood of Jesus Christ, his Son, cleanseth us from all sin."

Truly the love of God outlasted the sin of man, and now the broken love cord, severed by Satan has been salvaged by the Savior.

CHAPTER 2

VICTORY THROUGH CALVARY

Let the wicked forsake his way and the unrighteous man his thought, and let him return unto the Lord and he will have mercy upon him, and to our God for he will abundantly pardon. Isaiah 55:7

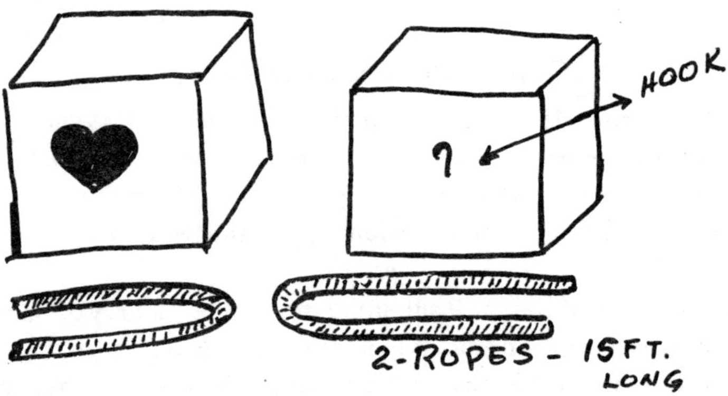

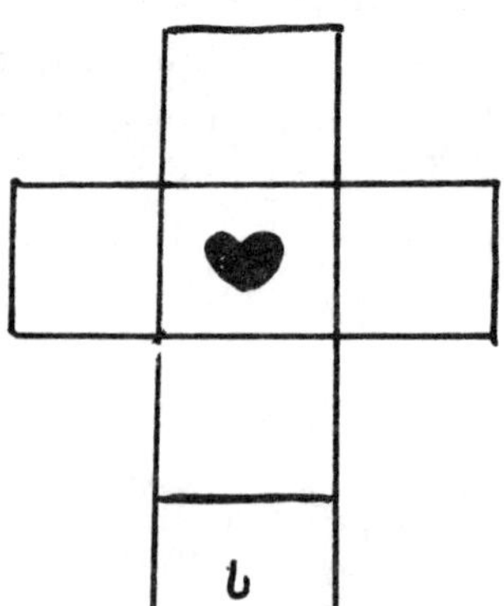

PROPERTY

Two lengths of rope, each 15 feet long, plywood, wire, rubber bands, a playing card and other paper objects.

PREPARATION

Construct a box with plywood squares 5 X 5 inches. Hinge these together in cross shape using cloth for hinges. Glue a red heart on front of the box and put a wire hook on the back to hold the ropes. Make a dummy cigarette and cut out a whiskey bottle from paper and have pieces of white, green, red, yellow and blue paper. Put all of these in the box.

PROCEDURE

Select three helpers, one to be back of the ropes and the other two to hold the ends of the ropes. Double each rope at the center and tie the double loops into a single loose knot. Place the loops over the wire hook.

During the lesson show all the objects in the box. Let the boy behind the ropes hold the box with his arms above the ropes. Take a single rope from each rope holder and bring the ropes behind the back of the boy and tie a single knot at his back and give each rope holder an end of rope, now crossed. Later in the lesson have the boy behind the ropes lift the box, which has been turned into a cross by removing the rubber bands. As he lifts the cross from the wire hook, he will be free with the ropes behind him.

PRESENTATION

I have three helpers, and John, the middle boy is going to walk right through this rope. You know, of course that John is not married and has never had a knot tied, but I am going to tie him up today.

BUTCH HAD MANY BAD HABITS

The boy I am going to talk about is not John. This boy did many things John would not do. I will call him Butch.

He was 18 years old. Because of his many bad habits

he lived a defeated life, and like John, he was on the wrong side of the rope, but we are going to get him on the right side.

HEART SURGERY

Let's operate on his heart and see what's wrong. (Open the box and remove the objects one by one).

Butch told white lies. (Hold up object as you progress). He cursed a blue streak, was green with envy, got red with anger, was cowardly with a yellow streak in time of temptation, he gambled with cards, smoked cigarettes and took the whiskey bottle as his best friend.

HALF REMEDY

He knew he was in great trouble and recalled a Bible verse he had learned in Sunday School, but he could remember only the first half of the verse. It was "Let the wicked forsake his way." He decided he would do that. He gave up his bad habits but he still was not free and had no peace. Satan now worked overtime on him and bound him even tighter. (Take one end of rope from each holder and bring ropes around John's body and tie a single but loose knot behind him. Then hand the now opposite ends back to the rope holders).

THE EMPTY HEART

Butch now had an empty heart and was miserable. What he didn't know was that you must put something else into that empty heart. (Let the box drop into the shape of a cross by removing the rubber bands).

Butch was really troubled. He was like the man who said, "I could swim if it wasn't for all this water." He was like the magician who could pull rabbits out of a hat but couldn't pull habits out of a rat. Butch needed Jesus. Giving up his bad habits would help his future but it wouldn't pay for his sins of the past. He needed not only a life saver, but also a life giver.

THE FINAL VICTORY

Then he met his Sunday School teacher. She told him she was glad he had given up his bad habits, but that he needed to have his past sins taken care of too and that those scars would remain and only a full surrender to Jesus and his forgivenes would give him peace and freedom.

The teacher told him if he really wanted to be a true follower he must take up the cross and follow him, by telling others, by praying, by reading the Bible, by being faithful to the church, by giving and by taking Jesus with him where ever he went and that when he did all that he would be free.. She gave him this verse, "If any man will come after me, let him deny himself and take up his cross and follow me." (Matth. 16:24). (Have John lift the cross from the hook and walk free of the ropes).

Then Butch remembered the verse he had forgotten. It said, "Let the wicked forsake his way and the unrighteous man his thoughts and let him return to the Lord and the Lord will have mercy upon him and will abundantly pardon." (Isaiah 55:7).

CHAPTER 3

FOUR STEPS TO FREEDOM

If the Son therefore shall make you free, ye shall be free indeed. John 8:36

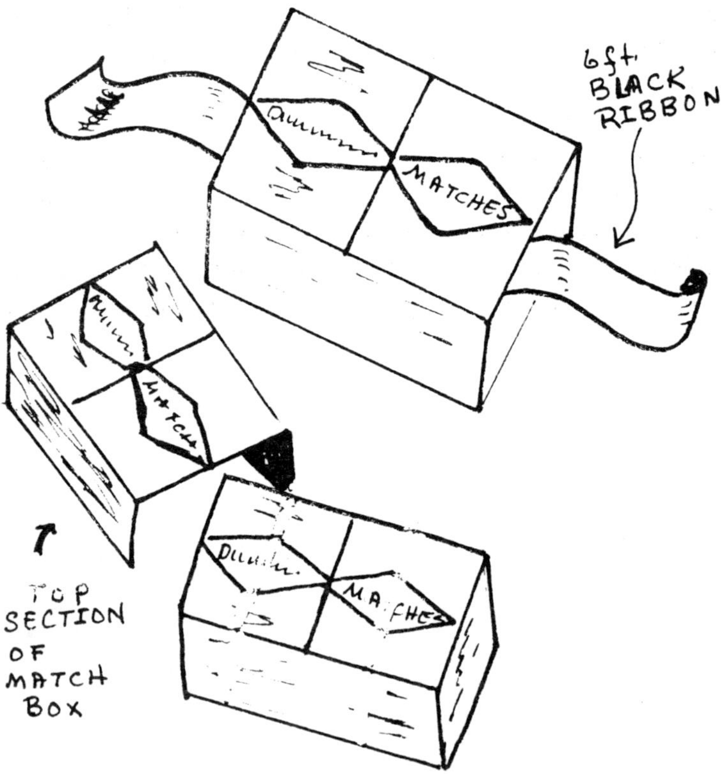

PROPERTY

Two safety match boxes, six feet of black ribbon and a handkerchief with a cross hand drawn on it with a marker.

PREPARATION

Take cover of one match box and remove the bottom section. Lay ribbon on top of box and place fake cover over the box over the ribbon and hold the assembly in place while you give the lesson.

PROCEDURE

Call for two helpers and have each of them hold one end of the ribbon. Place handkerchief over the assembly and remove the fake cover with the handkerchief, holding the box and ribbon with the free hand. Then show the box to be free from the ribbon

PRESENTATION

Peter was Herod's prisoner. (Acts 12:4). He was placed in a dungeon and 16 guards were assigned to watch over him, day and night, to prevent any attempt to escape. In addition, heavy chains were put around him. He was sentenced to death for preaching the gospel. His execution was to take place in a day or two. His friend James had already been put to death with a sword a day of two before.

THE DELIVERANCE OF PETER, PAUL AND JESUS

In the middle of the night the Angel of the Lord came and snapped off the chains and stupified the guards with sleep and then opened the big iron gate of the prison so Peter could pass through, freed from his imprisonment. (Acts 12:7).

Paul also was a prisoner many times. He and Silas, his preaching partner, were in prison at Philippi. At midnight, as they sang praises, God sent an earthquake that rumbled the gates ajar and all the prisoners escaped and Paul and Silas were free. Then they preached to the jailor and he and all his family became followers of Jesus. (Acts 16:30-34).

Paul was delivered from his persecutors many times. Once he escaped over a wall in a basket. (Acts 9:23-25).

He told the Corinthian Church about his hardships.(2 Cor. 11:23--28).

Jesus also became a prisoner to death and he was put in a borrowed tomb, but God delivered him even from this imprisonment and bondage and he came out of the tomb on the third day after his entombment.

If God was able to free Peter from prison and Paul and Silas from the jail at Philippi and Jesus from the tomb of death, don't you think he can free you from the sins and bad habits you may be chained with ?

YOU MAY BE A PRISONER

This little box represents you. It is a prisoner on the black, sinful, Satanic ribbon . This is somewhat like you. You may be a prisoner in a dark dungeon, chained by the habits you would like to get rid of.

THE FOUR STEPS TO FREEDOM

Jesus has already completed his part of the work to free you and he now invites you to do your part. When he died on the cross he said, "It is finished." (John 19:39)

The cross is a love picture with its top pointing to heaven and its arms saying, "Come, come, come and whosoever cometh I will not cast out." (John 6:37).

I will show you how you can come. There are four simple steps. They are all wrapped up together as though they were just one step and they all happen at once.

(Drape the handkerchief over the box). Jesus said he came to seek and to save the lost. (Matth. 18:11) (not in some modern versions, but true). The first step is to REPENT or be sorry for your past sins and turn from them, (Isaiah 55:7).

The second step is to BELIEVE in Jesus so firmly that you would be not only willing to live for him but also to die for him. (Acts 16:31).

The third step is to CONFESS him. That is what the Ethiopian Treasurer did when Philip preached Jesus unto him. (Acts 8:37). Rom. 10:9-10 says, "That if thou shalt confess with thy mouth the Lord Jesus and believe in thine heart . . . thou shalt be saved."

The fourth step is to RECEIVE Jesus. You let your heart become a home. You answer his knock and let him not to be a guest, but the new owner. (John 1:12). Having done this you will be free. (Remove the handkerchief and fake cover and show the box now to be free from the black ribbon). (If you want to add to the lesson, hide slips in the box, designating sins of the children. Remove and tear them up).

CHAPTER 4

THE REPENTANCE CHAIN

Let the wicked forsake his way . . . and return to the Lord, and he will have mercy and abundantly pardon

(Is. 55:7).

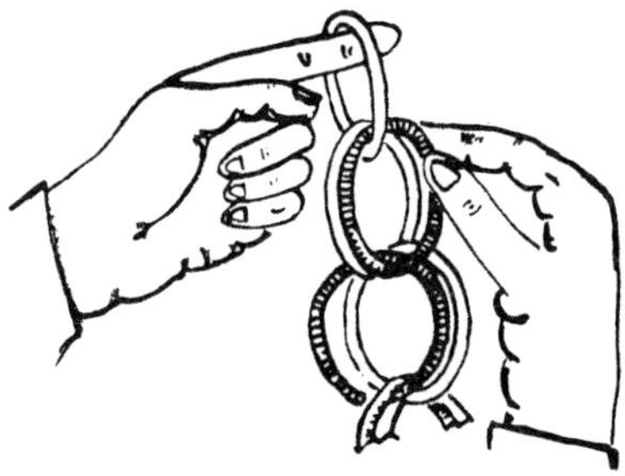

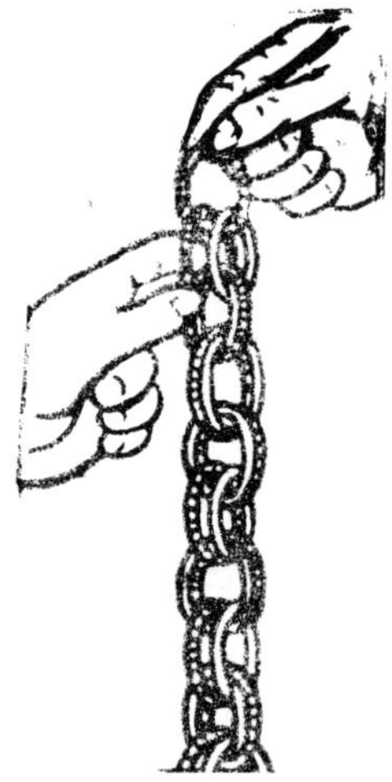

PROPERTY

24 large rings, such as are used for loose leaf note books, preferably those without hinges.

PREPARATION

Make two single chains. These are designated as Chain A and B. and the links 1, 2, 3,etc.

Hold link B-1 or top ring in right hand. Link A-1 into B-1. Then link A-2 into B-2. Then A-3 into B-3 and then A-4 into B-4. Follow this order until chains are completed

Hold B-1 in right hand on your right side throughout construction. When chain is completed you will have a single ring on top and another on the bottom of the chain.

PROCEDURE

Hold B-1 which is the top single ring in right hand. Hold A-1 in left hand and drop B-1 and it will appear to climb down the chain. Give chain a quarter turn counter-clockwise.Take single ring in right hand and drop it. Be sure before dropping it that each hand is holding a complete chain. You can test this by raising chain in left hand. If chain is not completely free on the other chain, you are not starting in the correct position or there is a mistake in the construction. If construction is right, by turning the chain a quarter turn each time it will be foolproof.

Then paint the bottom single ring black and you are ready for the lesson.

PRESENTATION

Some boys and girls allow a lot of bad habits to rule their lives. They become slaves and their habits become their masters.

Many believe that by giving up their bad habits, one by one, they can become conquerors and by so doing they become candidates for eternal life in heaven.

Since they are slaves and their sins are their masters, they are like this chain. They, like this black ring are on the bottom and all their habits or sins are on top of them, holding them down. They decide to drop their habits and climb to the top. (Drop one ring).

THE FAILURE OF SELF SALVATION

Aha, look where the black ring came to. It is starting to climb to the top. It is one step on the way to victory. Let's help it all we can. We will drop another habit. (Drop another ring). Hey, what happened, the black ring is on the bottom again. Maybe we did it wrong. Let's try again. There now it is on the way up again. (Continue dropping a ring from the top, each time giving the chain a quarter turn and changing the chain from one hand to the other).

THE PLAN THAT DID NOT WORK

That black ring is having a problem. It never will get to the top for it has never gone any higher after all these tries than it did the first time. I think there must be a better way to get that black ring to the top. I want you to help me decide the best way to get the black, bottom ring where the top ring is.

GOD'S WAY IS THE ONLY WAY

The black ring stands for sin and there is only one way to deal with it and that is God's way. We cannot get rid of the guilt of sin by just giving it up, any more than we can pay the grocery bill by assuring the grocer that we have now reformed and will never cheat him again because we are now honest.

The grocer will say, "But what about the debt you already owe me?" You see, boys and girls, just giving up your bad habits will not pay for your past sins.

But when we do it God's way, he will not only take us into his family and make us his children, but he will forgive the past sins we have committed and he will blot them out as a thick cloud and then the guilt will be gone. It will be like starting life all over again with a clean slate. He says it is like being born all over again. (John 3:3).

Paul says we become a new creation. "If any man be in Christ Jesus, he is a new creation, old things are passed away and all things are become new." (2 Cor. 5:17).

DO YOU KNOW THE WAY?

God tells us how to get the black ring of sin to the top where it should be. Can any of you tell me the easiest way? I tried it my way but the black ring did not climb to the top so I wonder if any of you can tell me the easiest way to get the bottom ring where the top one is.

REPENTANCE THE PATHWAY TO PEACE

Ah, you are pretty smart. You say the best way is to turn the whole chain upside down or turn it around. (Turn chain upside down so the bottom ring is now on top of the chain). This is what God wants us to do with our bad habits. When we do that we become masters and the bad habits become slaves.

God said, "Let the wicked forsake his way and the unrighteous man his thoughts . . . and let him return unto the Lord . . . and he will abundantly pardon. (Is. 55:7).

That is exactly what REPENTANCE is. It is to turn your life around and go the other way. That is why I call this the REPENTANCE CHAIN.

AN OBJECT LESSON ON REPENTANCE

An elderly minister attended an Assembly and a young minister spoke on REPENTANCE, giving the Greek words and Seminary explanation of what repentance is. When he was finished the old minister begged permission to explain repentance. He went to the platform and hobbled across it saying, "I'm going to hell, I'm going to hell, I'm going to hell." Then he stopped suddenly and turned about face and said happily and walked in the other direction across the platform and said, "I'm going to Heaven, I'm going to Heaven, I'm going to Heaven."

When he returned to his seat the audience knew that Repentance is being so sorry for your sins that you will forsake them and turn around and go the other way and never go back to them.

Before he met Jesus as Savior, Zaccheus was grasping for money in a dishonest way, but when he had his encounter with Jesus, he gave back what he had falsely gained and gave half of the rest to the poor. (Luke 19).

No matter what your sins of the past have been, God's grace is greater.

A PERSIAN PROVERB

There is no saint without a past and there is no sinner without a future.

CHAPTER 5

TRYING AND TRUSTING

I have blotted out, as a thick cloud, thy transgressions, and as a cloud thy sins; return unto me, for I have redeem- thee. Isaiah 44:22

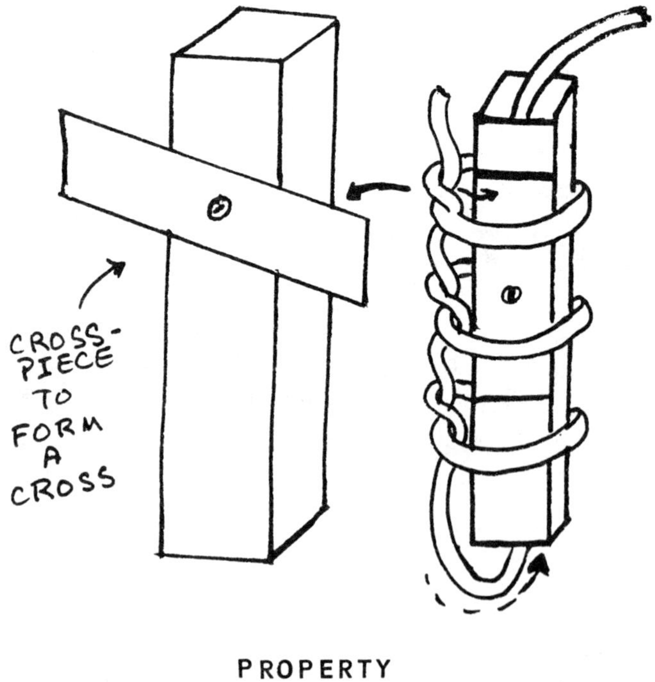

PROPERTY

Plywood, brads, a small bolt and 10 feet of soft rope.

PREPARATION

Construct a square box, 15 inches long and 2 inches square. Add a cross piece to one side, pivoting it to the assembly so it can be turned into a cross.

PROCEDURE

Tie three identical knots around the box and during the lesson slide them down below the cross piece. Thread the end of the rope at the lower end of the cross, through the box, carrying the knots into the box with it. In this manipulation the knots will be dissolved as they enter the cross and as you gently pull the end of the rope out of the upper end of the cross.

PRESENTATION

Sins are like the letters on the school blackboard. When the erasure is swished over the blackboard the letters have gone and no one knows where they have gone and no one remembers what they were. This is somewhat the way God says he will blot out our sins.

CHILDHOOD SINS

This box represents your life. Before you got very old, many things entered to mar that life. God calls them sin, and these sins come very early in life.

(Tie a knot around the box as shown). The sins that fasten themselves on a child's life may be lies, cheating, stealing, disobedience, anger, talking to parents disrespectfully, jealousy, taking God's name in vain, etc.

MIDDLE AGE SINS

This continues as you get older and into middle life. (Tie a second knot exactly in the same progression as the first knot).

The older you get, the harder it will be to get rid of those sins because sins become a way of life like breathing and eating and sleeping. They become a part of your nature.

Sins are like a calm sea that on the surface looks ever so peaceful, but underneath are the strong currents and undertow. They are like the peaceful woods that quiet and calm the troubled mind, but underneath the woodland carpet are the many insects and crawling creatures and all manner of dangerous living things that are unseen.

OLD AGE SINS

(Tie a third knot in the same progression). All through life, from childhhod to old age, sins come and an inner voice continues to warn that there are knots of sin entanging your life in the form of bad habits, and that there is a separation between you and God. You have come to know it and would like to do something about it. You would like to get untangled.

In your own strength you are TRYING to give up this sin and that, but somehow the guilt is like the strong turbulent current of the undertow of the sea and it continues to drag you away from God.

All seems peaceful on the outside, but on the inside there are inner feelings of sorrow that are like the tiny insects in the woods that sting and bite and poison and bring discomforts.

Quit TRYING. You are building a jail around yourself, and then becoming your own jailor. Noah's carpenters built the ark and themselves drowned in the flood. God tells us in his word, "By grace are ye saved through faith and that not of yourselves. It is the gift of God. Not of works, lest any man should boast." (Eph. 5:8-9).

SIN'S CURE

Let me give you the sure remedy for getting rid of your sins, no matter what time of life it is, whether childhood, middle life or old age.

(Push down the knots and swing out the cross piece). The remedy is already paid for. John 5:24 says, "He that heareth my word and believeth on him that sent me, hath everlasting life and shall not come into condemnation, but is passed from death unto life." Jesus also said in John 14:6, "I am the way . . . no man cometh unto the Father but by me."

God says not only that everyone must be saved, but that there is only one way to be saved. TRYING is not the way. TRUSTING is. It is through the cross that you can be saved. (Thread the bottom end of rope through the cross. Pull gently on the rope and the knots will be dissolved and the box will also be free.)

CHAPTER 6

BROKEN THINGS

". . . and viewed the walls of Jerusalem which were broken down . . ." (Neh. 2:13).

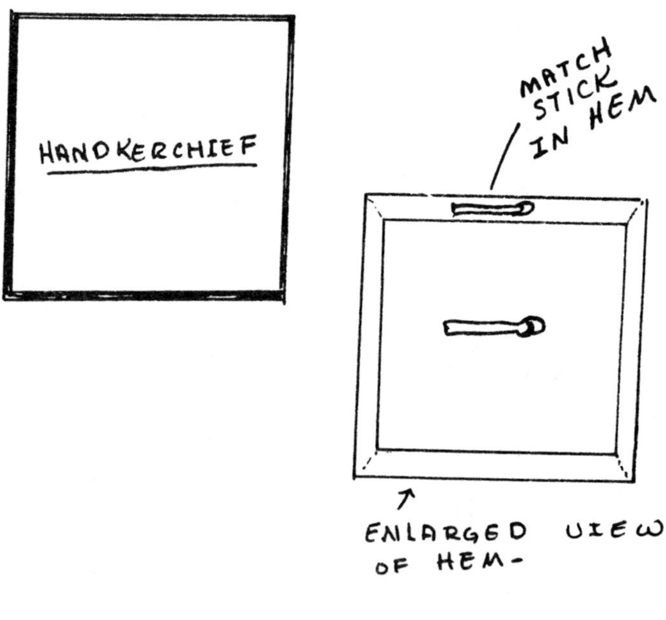

PROPERTY

A handkerchief and two wooden matchsticks.

PREPARATION

Break the heads off both matchsticks and insert one in the hem of the handkerchief.

PROCEDURE

Fold the second match in the handkerchief during the lesson and later have someone break the match in the hem. Unfold the handkerchief and show the match restored.

PRESENTATION

Many things get broken, like windows from a flying baseball, dolls by a careless girl mommy and hearts of parents by disobedient children.

Broken windows can be replaced by helpful daddies and broken doll heads by glue and broken toys by older friends. A tinker's shop had a sign on the window. It said, "We can mend anything but broken hearts". There is one who can outdo the tinker. It is Jesus. He said, "Come unto me all ye that labor and are heavy laden." (Matth. 11:28). Is. 61:1 says, "He hath sent me to heal the broken hearted."

There are many broken things mentioned in the Bible. Moses broke the stony tables of the law when he came down from smoky Mt. Sinat and found the people worshipping a molten calf. In disappointment and anger he dashed the tables to pieces, since the very first commandment said, "Thou shalt have no other gods before me." (Ex. 20).

BROKEN BREAD, PITCHERS AND A POTTER'S VESSEL

The broken bread at the Last Supper reminded the Twelve that the body of Jesus was to be broken on the cross. When he gave the broken pieces to his friends it was a reminder that they too might suffer. Some of them did, later, by crucifixion, stonings or the sword.

Then there were the pitchers, broken in the hands of Gideon's 300 soldiers as they blasted their trumpets. The call to battle of the trumpets and the clatter of the broken pitchers left fear and terror in the hearts of the Midianites. They fled under the impression that there must be a vast army. Thereby Gideon became a conqueror with only 300.

Then there was the broken vessel in the hands of the potter (Jer. 18:4). It was beautiful but marred. The potter did not throw it out the window. No, he crushed it and made it again from the same clay. This is like the new birth (John 3:3). You do not get new arms and legs or a new body. You are still the same boy and girl you have been but with a new spirit and a new outlook on a new life.

THE BROKEN MATCH

Let me illustrate it with this handkerchief and this match. I am going to put the match in the handkerchief. Then one of you will break the match to represent the broken things mentioned in the Bible.

(Place match in handkerchief and fold it in. Have someone break the match in the hem. Then show the match still unbroken).

When Moses broke the table of the law, God restored the law by writing it in the hearts of the people. Just about everybody knows the Ten Commandments, though they cannot repeat them from memory.. By nature we know when we break them because they have been so impressed on us.

RESTORATION BY RESURRECTION

When the body of Jesus was broken on the cross and he was laid in a dark and empty tomb, he was raised from the dead. We celebrate the resurrection on Easter Sunday.

When the walls of Jerusalem and its gates were broken down and lay in a heap, Nehemiah, the King's cupbearer led in the rebuilding of the walls and gates in the city where their dead were buried., because the people had a mind to work. Neh. Chapters 1 to 6

If broken things like broken pitchers, broken tables of stones, broken bread, broken pottery and broken walls and gates can be restored, your precious soul can be restored and reborn into a new life in Christ Jesus.

2 Cor. 5:17 declares that if any man be in Christ Jesus, old things are passed away and all things are become new.

GOD CAN RESTORE A BROKEN LIFE

Have your walls and gates been broken down and has sin invaded your life? Have you become a broken vessel because of carelessness and bad habits and you have stubbornly not allowed the divine potter to make you again?

Have you trampled under foot the broken tables of the law and not allowed God to write them in your heart? Does the clank of the broken pitchers and the blast of the trumpets drive fear into your heart and you have become a coward unwilling to face the sacrifices of a surrendered life?

Take heart. If Christ is for us, who can be against us ? (Rom. 8:31).

CHAPTER 7

THE FOREVER BOOK

But the Word of the Lord endureth forever.
(1 Pet. 1:25).

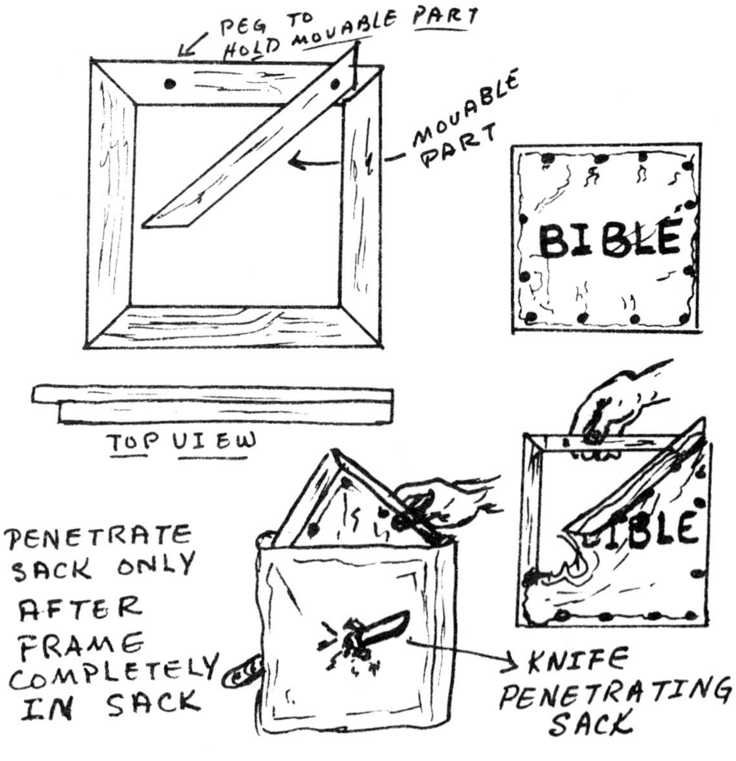

PROPERTY

Material to build a wood frame, a handkerchief, a magic marker, thumb tacks, a knife and a paper hat bag.

PREPARATION

Build a square frame the size of a handkerchief. Add an extra piece on one side, pivoted on one end so it can swing down,carrying the handkerchief with it. Print the word BIBLE on the handkerchief and fasten one edge of the handkerchief to the pivoted arm and the opposite edge to the frame, with thumbtacks.

PROCEDURE

Put frame into the hatsack which can be made of wrapping paper if such a sack is not available. Hold the frame by the innocent pivoted arm edge. When the frame is in the sack, drop the arm. It will carry the handkerchief with it in a diagonal position so you can plunge the knife through the sack without damaging the handkerchief.

Reach in and bring the pivoted arm back into place and withdraw the frame, showing the BIBLE to be unscathed.

PRESENTATION

God's workshop is the world he made. When he had completed his creative task, climaxing it with the creation of man, he provided a manual of operation for man to live by. It is called the BIBLE.

THE RULE BOOK MUST BE OBEYED

The BIBLE is like a telescope through which we can see God at close range, but some reverse the telescope and see him as very small and far off in the distance.

The rules in the BIBLE manual of man must be obeyed or we become like the man who bought a washing machine for his wife. The manual said so much water should be used at a certain temperature, and so much soap must be added and the clothes must be washed for so many minutes and then the clothes would come out clean. But this man did it his own way. He used less water at a lower temperature and less soap and ran the washer for less time, and the result was the clothes came out still soiled and dirty.

Because God knows the importance of the rule book for man's successful journey through life, he will never let it be destroyed.

GOD'S ARMOUR OF PROTECTION

There are three agents to guide and to preserve and help the Christian to grow.. They are the BIBLE, THE SACRIFICIAL BLOOD OF THE SON, and FIRE, sometimes called trials, but that FIRE is always ignited by the Holy Spirit, and for a purpose which may be unknown to you.

The BIBLE is like a refiners fire. Put a cold, black poker in the flame, and soon it becomes pink with heat, and like the fire in which it was bathed. As we soak up the Word of God, we become like its author and teacher.

So, of necessity God will never permit these agents, the the BIBLE, the blood of his Son and the Spirit to be destroyed. They are forever protected in the armour of his hand.

Let's put it to a test. Here is the BIBLE and here is the protective armour.

(Put the frame in the sack, holding the movable arm in place as it nestles against the frame.)

GOD, THE GUARDIAN OF HIS WORD

There are many destructive forces. Here is a knife, but what is a knife against the Sword of the Spirit? (Heb. 4:12).

The Sword of the Spirit, which is the Word of God is sharp and powerful. The knife has but one edge but the Sword of the Spirit has two and becomes more than a match for any weapon of destruction.

God has promised victory for the BIBLE over any attack against it. The attacker might be as powerful as the giant Goliath, but off in the distance, God has his little David with his sling and pebbles, ready for the onslought. The Watch Towers of heaven are on constant guardto see that the BIBLE will not be destroyed. The promise of God about it is as sure as the rainbow in the heavens which assures us from time to time that destruction will never come to the earth by flood. Likewise no force will ever destroy the Bible.

SCRIPTURAL PROMISES

(Plunge knife through the sack several times and pull out the frame and show that there was no destruction).

Matth. 5:18 says, "Till heaven and earth pass, one jot or tittle shall in nowise pass from the law till all be fulfilled." 1 Pet. 1:24,25 says, "For all flesh is as grass and the glory of man as the flower of grass. The grass withereth and the flower thereof withereth away, but the Word of God endureth forever."

"Being born again, not with corruptible seed but of incorruptible by the Word of God which liveth and abideth forever." (1 Pet. 1:23)."The grass withereth, the flower falleth, but the Word of God shall stand forever." (Isaiah 40:8). Jeremiah said, "Eat the Word." So, boys and girls, begin each day by reading the BIBLE, spend each day obeying the BIBLE and you will end each day and your very life by praising the keeper of the BIBLE for such a wonderful rule book that has brought you to such a glorious eternal home.

CHAPTER 8

THE MAN OF MIRACLES

And the Lord said unto him . . . . I have caused thee to see it with thine eyes, but thou shalt not go over thither.
(Deut 34:4)

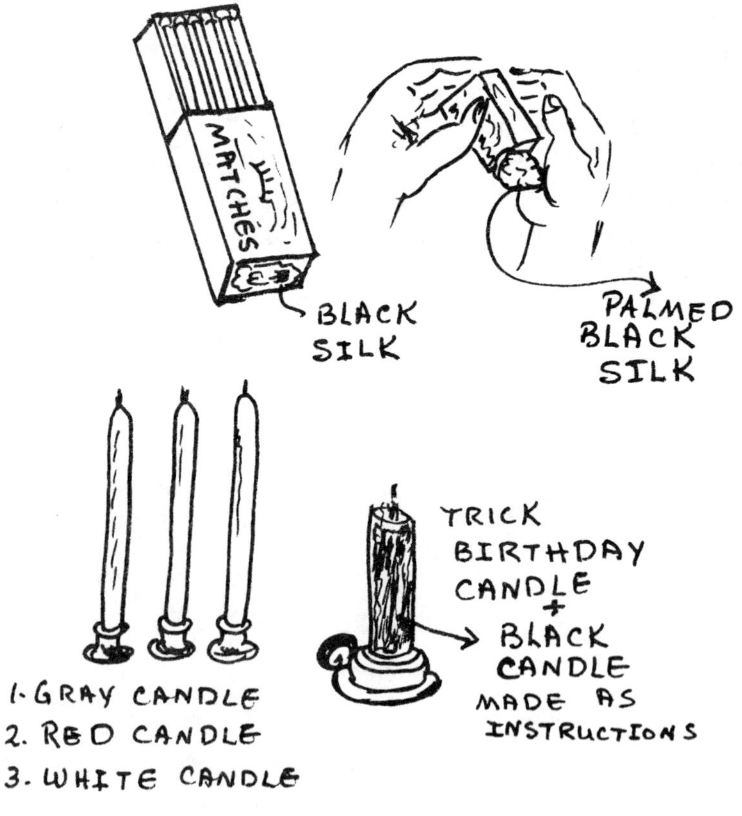

PROPERTY

A box of safety matches, three candles, gray, red and white. four candle holders, a dowel, a black silk and a trick birthday candle that lights itself repeatedly after it has been blown out. These are available in some variety stores.

PREPARATION

Have the box of matches half open. Crowd the black silk into the runway of the half open box, so when closed, the silk will drop into the hand. Drill a small hole in the end of the dowel and insert the birthday candle. Paint the dowel black and put dowel and candles in the holders.

PROCEDURE

During the lesson, light the candles, the gray for the Acacia bush, the red for the Red Sea and the white for the Rock of Horeb that became a fountain. Close the match box and push the silk into your free hand. At the proper time light the birthday candle. After about 30 seconds blow it out. Shortly it will re-light itself. Repeat several times.

PRESENTATION

I am going to play with fire. I do not advise you to do so. Fire can be harmful but also helpful. It can burn cities to ashes. It can also make hamburgers and hot dogs tasty and keep us warm in the winter and heat water for our showers. God used fire many times to accomplish his work. He used a coal of fire in the hands of an angel to put on the lips of Isaiah, the man of unclean lips. (Is. 6). It was in the midst of fire and smoke that God gave Moses the table of the ten commandments on Mt. Sinai. (Ex. 19:18). (Ex. 26: 1:18). (During this time be lighting some of the matches).

Malachi said the Savior would come as a Refiner's fire. (Mal. 3:1-2) The Forerunner of Christ, John The Baptist, when he announced the coming of the Savior, said, "He will baptize you with theHoly Ghost and with fire"(Matth.4:11-12).

It will be with fire that God will deal with those who have rejected his Son. (2 Thess. 1:8).

THE BURNING ACACIA BUSH

I want to explain about three episodes in the life of Moses. The first was while he was shepherding the sheep of his father-in-law, Jethro. One day a thorny Acacia bush caught fire, and yet it did not burn up. While Moses stood wondering and gazing at it, God spoke to him and appointed him to lead his ensalved fellow Israelites out of Egypt. (Ex. 3:2). Moses made excuses but God assured him he would be his constant guide. (Light the gray candle to represent the Acacia bush.

THE RED SEA

The second episode was when God saw the Israelites trapped on the wrong side of the Red Sea, with Pharaoh's army in hot pursuit. (Ex. 14:28).

Moses was commanded (Ex. 24:16) to lift his rod which was like a shepherd's staff,and part the water of the Red Sea. (Light the red candle). He parted the waters like your mother parts your hair. The people walked over on dry land.

THE ROCK OF HOREB

The third episode was at the Rock of Horeb in the wilderness of Zin. (Num. 29:11). It was a dry and thirsty land and the tongues were hanging out of the mouths of both animals and people, dying from lack of water.

At the command of the Lord, Moses struck the Rock of Horeb and it became a gushing fountain. The wildernes was a white, rocky land so I will light the white candle.

SO NEAR AND YET SO FAR FROM THE PROMISED LAND

Now God had a surprise for Moses, an unpleasant one. He told Moses he would not be permitted to go into the Promised land. God took him to Mt. Nebo so he could see it. Moses had failed to give God the glory in some of his miracles, and God closed the door against him. (Close match box and let the silk fall into your hand). It was a black picture for Moses. He was so near and yet so far. He died on Mt. Nebo in the heights of Pisgah, we know not where he was buried. (Deut. 34).. (Light and blow out candle in 30 seconds).

This did not mean that it was the end of spiritual life for Moses. Only his body died and was buried. Like this candle, his soul showed life, just like yours will after your body dies. The soul is eternal and will find its way to God's special place Jesus has gone to prepare for it.

Death does not end all. It is the beginning of a new life. You can see the body but not the soul. You can see every bone by the X Ray. You can see inside the stomach with a gastroscope, and inside the lungs with the bronchoscope and inside the bladder witha cystoscope, but there is no instrument to see the soul. Yet its value is greater than the whole world. (Matth. 16:26).

CHAPTER 9

THE RIGHT FOUNDATION

And the rain descended and the floods came and the winds blew and beat upon that house and it fell not for it was founded upon a rock. (Matth. 7:25).

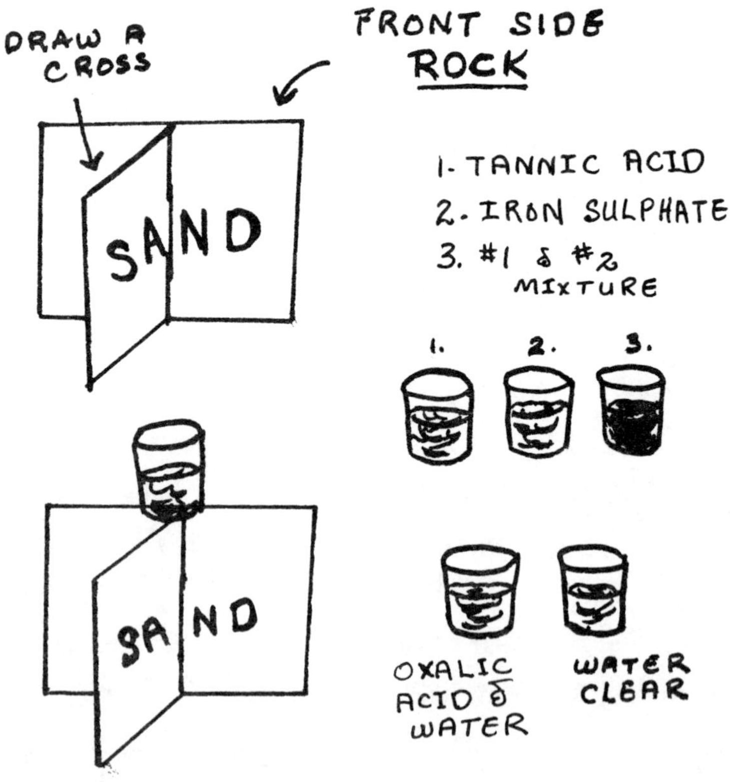

PROPERTY

Three glasses, dry chemicals from the drug store, Tannic Acid, Iron Sulphate and Oxalic Acid and two identical cards of fairly heavy stock.

PREPARATION

Put a pinch of Tannic Acid and a pinch of Iron Sulphate in one glass and several pinches of Oxalic Acid in another and add a little water to this glass. Put plain water in the third glass. If the chemicals are difficult to get, the lesson can be given without the chemicals

Glue half of one card to the center of the other card and fold it back as shown. Card will now stand by itself and a glass can be placed on it. It is best if you and object are elevated on stage or platform.

Print SAND on flap side of card and a cross with the flap folded in the opposite direction. Print ROCK on the other or plain side of card.

PROCEDURE

During the lesson, pour a half glass of water into the glass that has the Tannic Acid and Iron Sulphate. It will turn black. Then pour the black water into the Oxalic Acid glass and it will clear the black.

After showing both sides of the card, secretly turn out the flap while it is resting on the table, but holding the card as though to balance it. Place the glass with the two chemicals on the three edges of the flapped card. Finally let go of the cards to show that Jesus is the only safe foundation on which to build a life. Then dissemble and with the flap folded in the correct position, show the cross.

PRESENTATION

Jesus preached only one sermon and it is called The Sermon On The Mount, because it was delivered from a mountain side. (Matth. 5:2).

He concluded the sermon with a story of a man who built

his house on a foundation of SAND. When the storm began shedding tears for this foolish man and the teardrops fell in a torrential rain and the winds began to blow like Blow-Me-Down Popeye, the foundation was washed away and the house fell 'ker-plop.' This was meant to teach them not to build their lives on an insecure faoundation. (Show SAND side of card.)

Then he told about another man who built his house on a foundation of ROCK. When the winds and the rain beat against that house, it withstood the storm and the people within were safe because the house was on the right kind of foundation.

Paul advised the church of Corinth in 1 Cor. 3:10-11 that a wise masterbuilder is certain about the foundation and then added, "For other foundation can no man lay than that is laid, Christ Jesus."

THE STORM

I will let this glass serve as the house, because if it falls it will break like the house built on SAND. But we are going to build on ROCK. (Show ROCK side of card and secretly turn out the flap.)

Now I will build the house on ROCK and we will see if it can hold the house up and stand against the storm.

I can see the storm coming. It is beginning to rain and the clouds are turning black.(Pour clear water into the glass of Tannic Acid and Iron Sulphate. It will turn black.

Ah, the house stands against the storm because it is on the right foundation.

Now the storm is over. Everything must have an end, except a sausage. It has two ends. It is still raining but the clouds are clearing up. (Pour the black water into the Oxalic Acid and the water will become clear).

YOU ARE GOD'S HOUSE

Temptations are like storms that beat against the life. Here is the right foundation. (Show the cross). Did you know that your body is the house your life lives in? It is also the temple that God lives in. How careful we should be with God living in the same house we live in. Our language, our attitude towards our parents, our everything should be done and said, knowing that he hears and sees and notes all that we do and say.

I want my life to be built on the foundation of the one who can serve as my bodyguard when Satan attacks. He is the only one who ever controlled the winds and the waves of stormy Galilee when the boat with his friends aboard were fearful lest it should sink. They were not as brave as the man who couldn't swim. He said, "I will sink to the bottom and walk as fast as I can to the shoreline." This boat and these friends were four miles from the shore, so they cried for help. Jesus arose from this sleep and said, "Peace be still," and the storm was suddenly over and his friends said, "What manner of man is this that even the winds and the waves obey his will?" (Mark 4:39).

CHAPTER 10

CHRIST THE SUBSTITUTE

". . . the Lord hath laid on him the iniquity of us all."
(Is. 53:6).

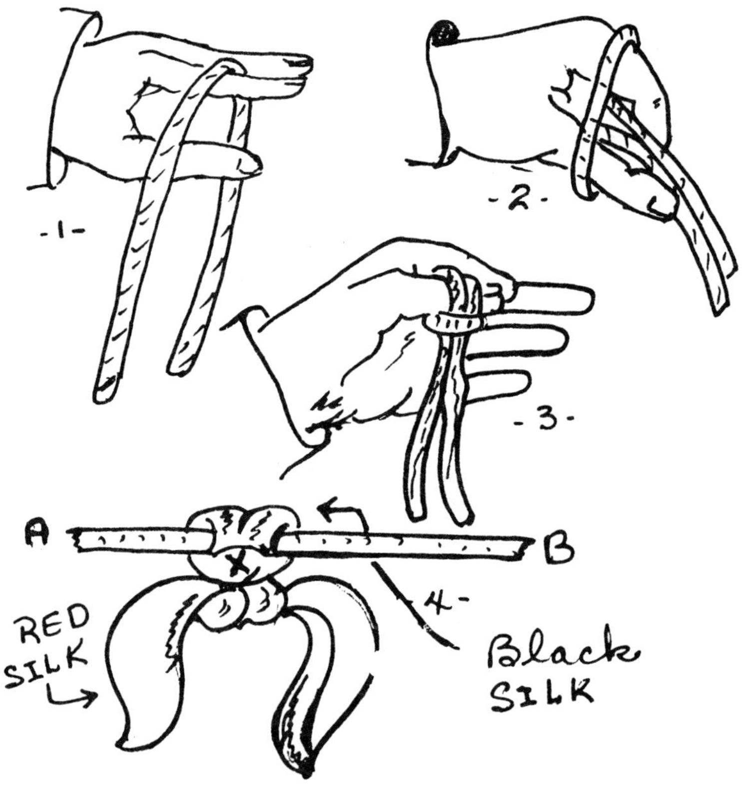

PROPERTY

A length of soft rope about 8 feet long, a black silk and a red silk.

PREPARATION

PRACTICE, PRACTICE, PRACTICE. Form a loop in the center of the rope as in Figs. 1,2 and 3. Tie a black silk in the loop where the thumb is as in Fig. 3. Pull on the rope at points A and B and this will flip the black silk into the position of Fig. 4

Tie the red silk with a double knot on the black silk, at point X of Fig. 4. Pull gently on the red silk and the black silk will slide off the rope, attached to the red silk.

PROCEDURE

During the lesson have two boys hold the ends of the rope and follow the instructions under PREPARATION.

PRESENTATION

This rope represents your life, boys and girls. I do hope your life will be longer than this short rope, but God has made no promise about how long this life may be. There are long and short graves in every cemetery.

This black silk will show what has come into your life in the way of bad habits which God calls sin. The red silk is a picture of Jesus who came to help us.

LIFE MAY BE SHORT OR LONG

There are long and short stories and God has said life is like a story or as a tale that is told. (Ps. 90:9). He also said our lives are like the grass and flower that wilt in the sun (Ps. 103:15) and like a swift ship that soon passes from the vision on the horizon and like the postman or mail man who soon disappears down the street. (Job 9:25-26).

SIN IS A DEBT

Here is a black silk. It stands for sin, such as comes into everyone's life. God says in Rom. 3:23, "All have sinned and come short of the glory of God. There is none righteous, no not one." Is. 53:6 says that all have gone astray like sheep, but that the Lord has laid on Jesus the iniquity or sin that has come into our lives.. When sin was hanging over us like a huge debt, far too big for us the ever pay, God solved that problem. He arranged for another to pay that debt for us. He did not send the angel Gabriel or the arch angel Michael or our father or mother or Pastor or Sunday School teacher to pay the debt, but he sent his own Son, the Lord Jesus.

John 3:16 says so, as well as many other versesin God's Word. Matth. 18:11 says Jesus came into the world to seek and to save that which was lost and John 10:10 says that he came that we might have life and have it more abundantly. That was like adding Green stamps to thepurchase already made. He said in Rom. 8:32, "He that spared not his own Son, but delivered him up for us all, how shall he not with him also freely give us all things?"

GOD'S PLAN FOR REDEMPTION

So Jesus came to the very heart of your problem and became the substitute payment for your sins and mine. (Having pulled on the rope to form a loop in the black silk, tie the red silk in the loop of the black silk).

You see what Isaiah meant when he said, "He hath laid on him the iniquity of us all" and what Paul meant when he said, "He hath made him to be sin for us (he who knew no sin that we might be made the righteousness of God in him" (2 Cor. 5:21).

Jesus did not come just to teach us as a friend. He came to reach us as a Savior. He did not come to tell us how bad we are but to remove the sin that made us bad.

I said the rope was like our life and the black silk was like our sins and the red silk was for Jesus who came to take the sins out of our life by taking them upon himself.

(Tie the red silk in the black silk). God has laid our sins on his Son, but that is not all. He removes them and takes them upon himself. They will be gone forever.

Here is your life. (Point to rope). Here is your sin. (Point to black silk). Here is your Savior. (Point to red silk). And here is your salavtion. (Pull on red silk and remove black, attached to the red.)

Jesus has taken your sins on himself, just as God said for he has laid on him the iniquity of us all. Since it is a gift, you can only lay claim to it by being willing to re-receive it. It is free for the asking.

CHAPTER 11

THE UNCERTAINTY OF LIFE

So teach us to number our days that we may apply our hearts unto wisdom. (Psalm 90: 7-8).

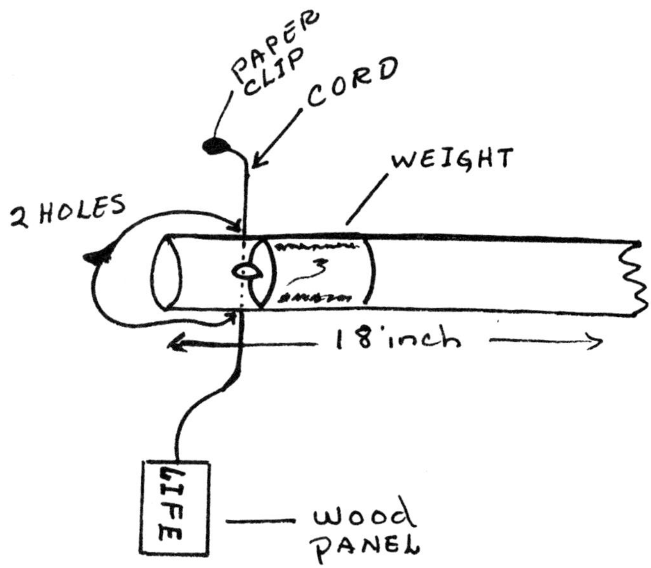

PROPERTY

An 18 inch length of chromed pipe, such as the plumbers use in bathrooms, a weight that will slide inside the pipe, a screw eye, a hard, smooth cord, a flat panel of wood, two corks and two paper clips.

PREPARATION

It may require machining to provide the iron weight that slides in the pipe. Solder the screw eye to the end of the weight. Drill holes opposite each other near the top end of the pipe. Put the cord through a hole and through the screw eye and out the other hole.

Attach a wooden panel to one end of the cord and print the word LIFE on the panel. Attach the paper clips to the ends of the cord to serve as stoppers. Put corks in both ends of the pipes. It may be necessary to put a hole in each cork to prevent a vacuum. The cord should be four times the length of the pipe.

PROCEDURE

Pull the cord to its full length, up and down, with the pipe tilted downward. Do this repeatedly during the lesson and the cord will get shorter and shorter.

PRESENTATION

God says in Hebrews 9:27 - "It is appointed unto man once to die." The Psalmist said in Ps. 90:7, "Teach us to number our days and apply our hearts unto wisdom." James 4:13 warns that we should not promise that we are going into a certain city today or tomorrow and plan to continue there to buy and sell for we do not know what is in store beyond the moment and that is why the Psalmist said, "Teach us to number our days" that we may act wisely during the days that may be left of our lives. The very last day could be TODAY. We have nothing to do with tomorrow. God has his own calender and clock.

Every day we live brings us one day closer to eternity and God alone knows the secret day and hour when each life shall come to a close or when Jesus will return. The knowledge of the day of death, as to when, where or how would only add unbearable anxiety to life. So his tender warning is "Be ye ready." This experience will come as a thief in the night.

HOW OLD MUST YOU BE TO DIE?

A little girl said, "Mother, how old do you have to be before you die?" The mother gave the girl a rope and instructed her to go to the cemetery and measure the graves and to tie a knot in the rope for each different length of grave she found. There were long and short graves, for children, parents and grandparents. So we must prepare today for what might come tomorrow.

No wonder the Psalmist said, "So teach us to number our days that we might plan wisely and have our loins girt and our lamps trimmed and our feet sandaled as the ancient Israelites did when they began their march to the Promised land.

When we reach that day, we will stand before God to give an account of ourselves. (Rom. 14:12). We may now be closer to that day than we think. We see canes and crutches and eye glasses and dentures and hearing aids because the day we were born we began to die and we have been dying ever since. If we were buildings instead of people we would have been condemned long ago. When we are called upon to appear before God he will be either our judge or our Savior. What he does with us hereafter will depend on what we did with him here.

MOODY'S MEMORIES

When the greal Evangelist and soul winner D.L.Moody lay dying he saw Heaven and he said, "Earth is passing away and Heaven is opening. This is my coronation day." A few moments later he received the crown of life.

As a young boy in New England he remembered that the village church bell tolled when someone died, and it always tolled out the number of years that person had lived. Sometimes it would toll five times and sometimes seventy five.

He shuddered each time at the tolling of the bell because he was not himself prepared to die. But when he came to Jesus and his sins were forgiven, he thought of death, not in fear and trembling but as a promotion or graduation day and like a discharge from the warfare of life.

DEATH IS NOT THE END BUT THE BEGINNING

The Apostle Paul spoke about death as the beginning of a new life. He said, "The time of my departure is at hand, I have fought a good fight, I have kept the faith. I have finished the race . . . henceforth there is laid up for me a crown of righteousness . . . " (2 Tim. 4:6). He further said in substance, "I am squeezed in between the walls of a narrow place, having a desire to live and at the same time to die which is far better."

Solomon summed it all up when he said in the 12th chapter of Eccles. "All of life is vain. Vanity of vanities, all is vanity. Let us hear the conclusion of the whole matter. Fear God and keep his commandments."

(During the entire lesson keep pulling the cord, and gradually letting it become shorter).

CHAPTER 12

THE SALVATION BOX

. . .though your sins be as scarlet, they shall be as white as snow . . . (Is. 1: 18).

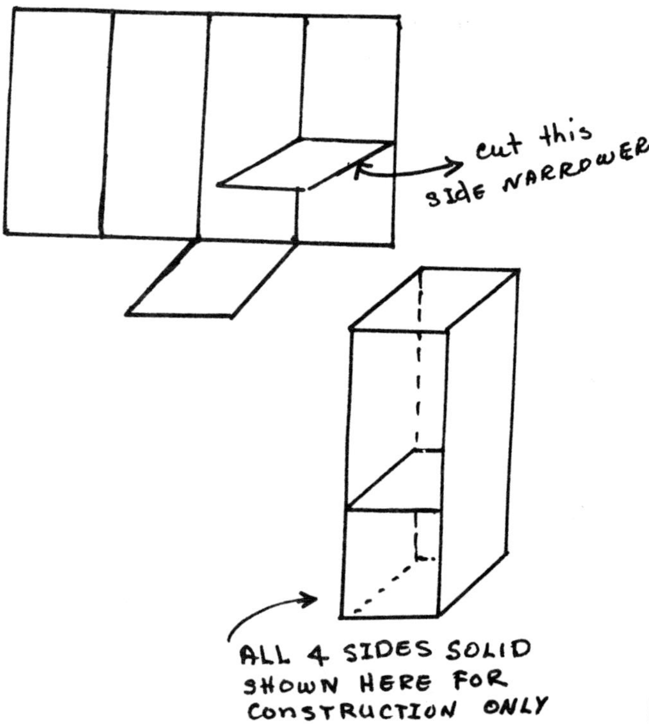

PROPERTY

Colored cardboard, gummed tape, a handkerchief and a marker.

PREPARATION

Build a box with cardboard and gummed tape, including the regular bottom. Before joining the ends of the box and completing the bottom, attach a shelf to one panel of the inside of box, several inches above the bottom. It should be ½ inch narrower on one side and should be finally attached to the other three panels to form a false bottom.

Cut colored cardboard discs, white, blue, red and black, a bit smaller than the width of the box and the space under the fake bottom. Draw a cross on the handkerchief.

PROCEDURE

Drop the four colored discs in the box as you give the lesson, tilting the box so the discs will fall through the narrow space at the side of the shelf. Later, place the handkerchief over the box, being sure the four discs are under the false bottom. Then turn the box upside down showing that all the sins have been blotted out.

The colored discs represent the sins of the children, the handkerchief the redemptive work of Christ and the box the salvation that comes when sins are laid on Jesus.

PRESENTATION

There are all kinds of sins, like anger, telling white lies, swearing, stealing, disobeying parents, etc.

I have a box here I will call my Salvation Box. I am going to put some sins in it. They will then be hidden from view so they could be called secret sins for they are hidden from parents, Sunday School teachers, Pastor, etc.

The trouble with secret sins is that they are never secret. God always knows all about them for secrets are not hidden from God. He has an all seeing eye and he never slumbers nor sleeps, but he is a merciful God. He knoweth our frame and remembereth that we are dust, and like a father pitieth his children, so the Lord pitieth them that fear him. (Ps. 103:13-14).

THE SIN OF ANGER

I have several round colored discs. Each color could stand for a sin. White for telling little white lies, blue for cursing a blue streak, red for anger and black for all the sins I did not mention. (Hold up each individual disc and drop each in the Salvation Box where strange things happen.) Peter was guilty of telling a lie so I will drop the white disc in. He also cursed so here goes the blue one in. He also got angry in the Garden of Gethsemane and cut off a man's ear, so I will drop in the red one. Here is the black one and that will be for all your sins and the many I have not mentioned.

Most children do not lie and steal and curse, but many do get angry. When you get angry and red in the face, you lose control of yourself and may harm someone or even yourself.

I had a friend who became so angry he beat his fist against the wall and broke his hand. He could not work for weeks, besides having a big doctor bill.

If you get angry easily and often, ask God to help you. The Bible says, "Let not the sun go down upon your wrath." (Eph. 4:26). That means you should get over your anger in a hurry, but better yet, do not get angry.

SINS ARE NOT MEASURED WITH A YARDSTICK

Sin is sin and there are no big and little sins in God's catalog, so the wages are all the same.

If you have lied once, you are a liar. If you have stolen once, you are a thief. If you have ever committed any sin, you are a sinner. (Place black disc in Salvation Box).

In spite of all the sins you have piled up in your life, God still loves you and to show you how much he loved you, he sent Jesus to remind you of that love. (Hold up the handkerchief). The Bible says, "God sent not his Son into world to condemn the world but that the world through him might be saved.

(Place handkerchief over the box. Remove the handkerchief and turn the box over to pour out the discs only to reveal that the sins have been blotted out).

Jesus wants to blot out your sins by taking them on himself. He has already paid for them. He came to seek and to save the lost. (Matth. 18:11). Is. 53:6 says "All we like sheep have gone astray, we have turned every one to his own way and the Lord hath laid on him the iniquity of us all."

Come to him today before you get any older and the burden of sin gets bigger and heavier. Now is the accepted time, today is the day of salvation. Let Jesus be like the Salvation Box.

The devil has many wiles and the latest wile is WAIT A WHILE. If you postpone today's responsibility to tomorrow, remember that TODAY is the TOMORROW you talked about YESTERDAY.

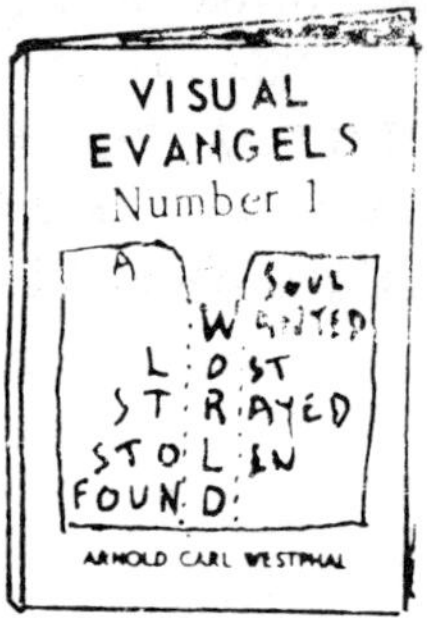

HAPPY SURPRISE JUNIOR OBJECTALKS
MAGIC WITH HOME-MADE STUFF
VISUAL EVANGELS NO. 1
VISUAL EVANGELS NO. 2
VISUAL EVANGELS NO. 3
VISUAL EVANGELS NO. 4
VISUAL EVANGELS NO. 5
VISUAL EVANGELS NO. 6
JUNIOR SURPRISE SERMONS NO. 1
JUNIOR SURPRISE SERMONS NO. 2

THE AUTHOR, NOW APPROACHING HIS 85TH YEAR IS STILL ACTIVE AS A PASTOR, SERVING VILLAGE GREEN SOUTHERN BAPTIST CHURCH IN HIS HOME TOWN.

IT IS HIS 6TH INTERIM PASTORATE LOCALLY.

HE HAS ACCEPTABLY USED VISUAL AIDS FOR THE CHILDREN EACH SUNDAY MORNING IN EACH OF THE CHURCHES

OTHER BOOKS AVAILABLE

By the same author

FOR OVER 50 YEARS THE POPULARITY OF THESE SURPRISE GOSPEL OBJECT LESSONS HAS NOT WANED. OVER 1,000,000 ARE NOW IN CIRCULATION IN ALL DENOMINATIONS

8 JACKETS
64 LESSONS

WITH OBJECTS
INCLUDED

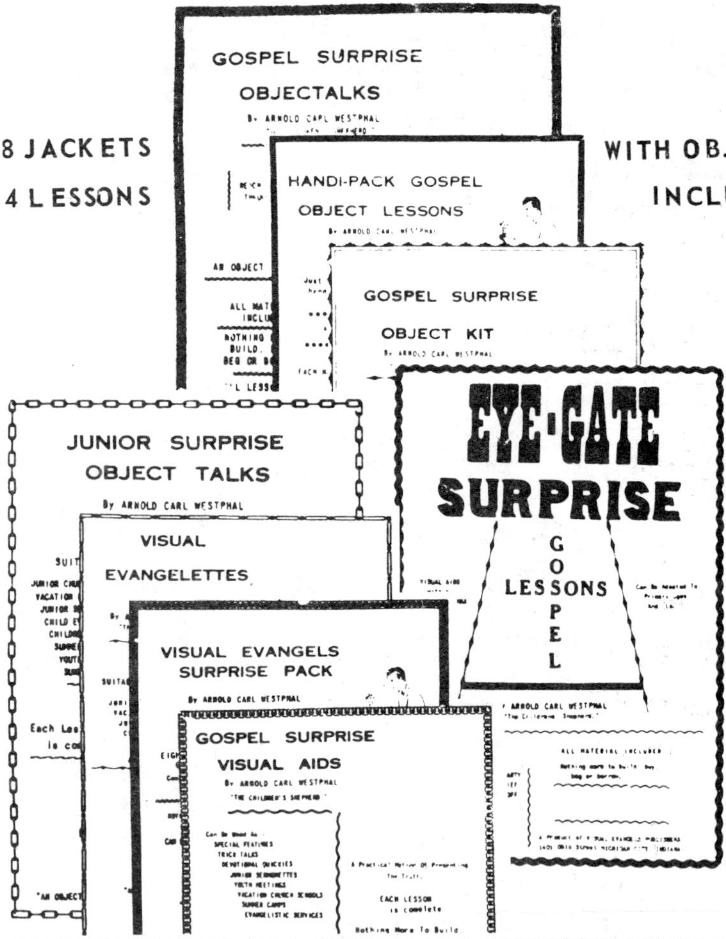

IF YOU ARE NOT A DO-IT-YOURSELFER, BUY THE SIX VISUAL EVANGEL BOOKS. DO NOT BUY BOTH FOR THE PACKETS ARE THE SAME MATERIAL IN BOOK FORM, WITH THE COPY MORE EXTENDED.